Elevate Yourself

By Evette Rose

Edition 1

ISBN: 9798875630873

Disclaimer

All information obtained from Evette Rose, or anything written or said by her, is to be taken solely as advisory in nature. Evette Rose and Metaphysical Anatomy™ will not be held personally, legally, or financially liable for any action taken based upon their advice. Evette Rose is not a psychologist or medical professional and is unable to diagnose, prescribe, treat, or cure any ailment. Anyone using the information in this book acknowledges that they have read and understand the details of this disclaimer. Evette can discuss the metaphysical explanations for psychological disorders but are unable to diagnose, prescribe, treat, or claim to cure any illnesses that require medical or psychiatric attention. The principles taught in Metaphysical Anatomy™ and in this book is based on Evette's life experiences and are guidelines and suggestions to support those seeking simple tools to improve their quality of life. By utilizing and using this book, the participant acknowledges that he/she assumes full responsibility for the knowledge gained herein and its application. Material in this book is not intended to replace the advice of a competent healthcare practitioner. The reader takes full responsibility for the way they utilize and exercise the information in this book.

Legal

All recordings and publications obtained from Evette Rose, or this book remain the intellectual property of the aforementioned and must not be used or reprinted in any way without the written permission of Evette Rose. Any unauthorized commercial use of Evette Rose's name, photograph, images, or written material is strictly prohibited and is in direct violation of rights.

ACKNOWLEDGMENTS

Thank you to each and every client or student that I have met for your insight, support, and willingness to share your life stories. I would not have been able to write this book without you! Thank you, Noemi Idang, for your unconditional support!

With Love,
Evette Rose

Also by the author

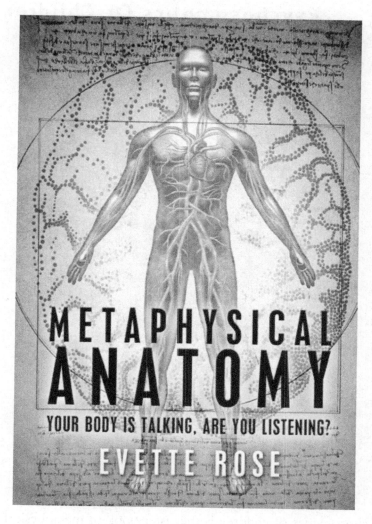

Metaphysical Anatomy is about 679 illnesses from A – Z. This book is so much more than the emotional components of each disease. Metaphysical Anatomy also includes step-by-step guide for identifying the origin of the disease process, whether it be in your ancestry, conception, womb, birth, or childhood. This book is equally valuable for experienced alternative healing practitioners, psychotherapists, hypnotherapists, personal development coaches and those interested in self-healing.

Psychosomatics Of Children
Your Ancestry is talking
Are you Listening?

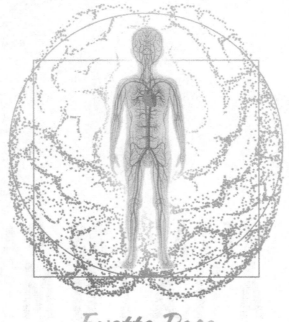

Evette Rose
METAPHYSICAL ANATOMY VOLUME 3

Psychosomatics of children is the sister book of metaphysical anatomy volume one. This book focuses on children's ailments and psychological challenges. Children have not had a full life yet. Therefore, ailments in their bodies are stemming from womb and ancestral trauma, which is unresolved. Not only is your body talking in this book, but your ancestry is talking, are you listening?

DECODING
Trauma

A DIFFERENT PERSPECTIVE ON TRAUMA

Evette Rose

Trauma Decoded. It's time to get back to who you really are! This book is for people who want to change their lives but don't know where to start or what steps to take first, because they have never looked at themselves before, or because they have tried everything else and failed so badly that they feel like a failure and it's easier not to try again than risk failing again, which would make them feel even more of a failure. You are not destined for failure! You are destined for greatness!

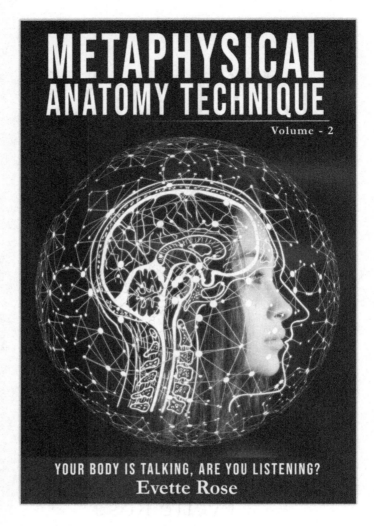

Metaphysical Anatomy Technique Volume 2 explains the core foundation and healing technique behind Metaphysical Anatomy Volume 1 which describes step-by-step guide for identifying the psychosomatic pattern related to 679 medical conditions. These conditions can be activated by circumstances in your present life, your ancestry, conception, womb, birth trauma, childhood, or adult life. Volume 2 teaches you the foundation of Volume 1 including a powerful healing technique. There is also an Online Healing Course that you can combine with Volume 1 and Volume 2.

"The Anxious Dialogue" is a self-help book that helps you get unstuck, live with more ease, and feel better. It's a workbook for your mind, heart, and nervous system. It's a quick read with tons of exercises to help you challenge your thinking patterns and change the way you respond to stressors in your life." It has exercises and practical advice that will help you stop your anxiety from controlling your life. You'll learn to identify the patterns and habits that keep your anxiety going, then choose new ways of thinking and behaving to replace them. You'll also be able to practice this new way of being immediately with fun, easy-to-use steps to help you relax and reduce stress.

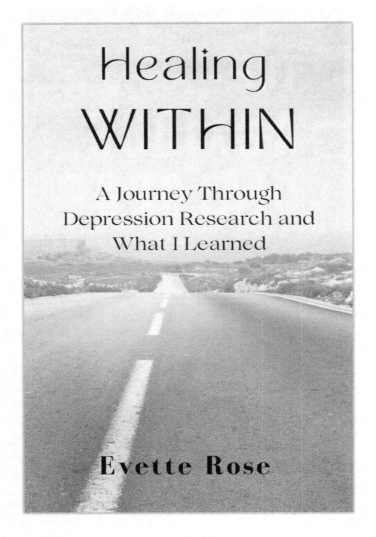

Depression can be a heavy, difficult-to-lift weight. It can sap your energy and make it hard to motivate yourself. But depression is a real condition that often requires treatment. There are many different types of depression, with various causes. Some people experience depression in response to a specific event, while others have ongoing, long-term problems that contribute to their depression. Depression can affect anyone, regardless of age, race, or gender. It's not always easy to recognize, but there are ways to get help.

"The Pain Puzzle" is a book about pain and how to deal with it. Chronic pain affects millions of people worldwide, but there's still so much we don't understand about it. Our goal for this book is to give you the tools you need to understand with your own pain, as well as share some of our findings from research on the topic." If you're suffering from psychosomatic pain, emotional pain, or any other type of ailment pain, "The Pain Puzzle" can help you understand your pain from a new perspective. The Psychosomatics of pain refer to the idea that our thoughts and emotions can contribute to pain. For example, someone who is constantly worrying about their pain may find that their pain gets worse. Our understanding of pain has come a long way, especially in my research. In this book, I will share my research regarding pain, chronic pain, and psychosomatic pain.

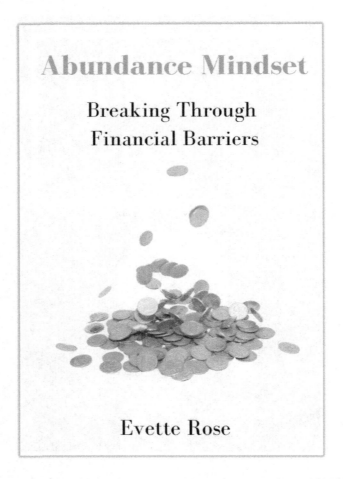

Address your abundance mindset to create prosperity and abundance. Manifest success and heal blocks to abundance with this powerful financial tool. Get clear about your values and ancestry to empower your financial future. Create awareness around your relationship to money for lasting change. This is a great guide to getting your money in order and becoming successful. Get blocks off your energy and start achieving your goals with this helpful guide to financial awareness. Heal your relationship with money and achieve abundance with this valuable guide to financial ancestry. Discover your values and manifest wealth with this enlightening guide to financial success. If you can resolve and release these issues, you will open yourself up to a more prosperous future.

"Boundary Breakthrough" is a self-help book that will help you reclaim your life. It's a guide to understanding and setting healthy boundaries and learning to say no when you need to. If you've ever felt trapped or held back by your relationships, this is the book for you. "It is relatable, and packed with information that will change your life for the better. If you're tired of feeling like you're constantly walking on eggshells, it's time to get your boundaries back! This book will help you set healthy limits and finally start living the life you deserve. build resilience and thrive in the face of adversity, this is the book for you!

"The Content Code" is a life-changing book that will show you how to be happy. It's packed with powerful techniques and strategies that will help you overcome unhappiness and trauma. You'll finally be able to find your purpose in life and achieve your birthright to happiness. This book is engaging, and easy to read - perfect for anyone who wants to start living a happier life today! It's a guide to overcoming trauma and negative associations that hold you back from happiness.

Navigating
Communication Blocks

A Journey in Understanding Communication

Evette Rose

"Navigating Communication Blocks" is a communication tool designed to help you become more effective and successful at communicating with others. It is based on the premise that most people have some sort of block when it comes to communicating effectively. By becoming aware of these blocks, you can resolve them and improve the way you communicate with other people. This will lead to better relationships, more success in your career, and greater happiness overall.

Elevate Yourself

Reclaiming Self-love

Evette Rose

"Elevate Yourself" is a book that will help you release your past self-sabotaging patterns, clear out your negative associations with yourself, heal your confidence, and more. This book is all about finding love for yourself, no matter what you've been through. It's about learning to forgive yourself for the things that have happened to you in the past or even recently. It's about letting go of old stories that keep you stuck. It's time to shine your light!

"Embrace the Heartbreak" is a guide for turning your life around after a relationship. It includes exercises that will help you discover the root of your problems and give you tools for moving forward with grace and ease. This book is for anyone who has ever questioned their self-worth or felt lost in love. This is a self-help book that helps you heal from heartbreak, divorce, relationship challenges, and abuse. It shows you how to manifest the love of your life and values into your life. This book helps you change the negative patterns in your life, such as sabotage and regret.

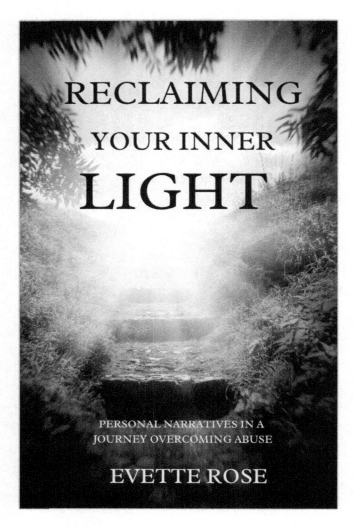

Are you tired of being abused? It's time to break the silence! I can relate because that person used to be me. In this book share my life story, the good the bad and ugly. Being raised in a violent home along with a drug addicted, alcoholic parent trying to navigate my way through what seemed to be the beginning of the end. "Reclaiming Your Inner Light" is here to help you heal from the trauma of abuse and become the confident person you were meant to be.

This true-life story is a must-read for people who have either experienced abuse or care about someone else who may be trapped in processing their childhood experiences. This book brings an empowering message of hope, healing and understanding to anyone who feels challenged by their past.

"Relationship Resolution" is a guide to healing relationships, trauma, anger in relationships and gaslighting. If you're dealing with a narcissist or controlling partner, this book has the solutions you need. Figure out your language for love, boundaries, dating, marriage, and more. Learn about the language of love and boundaries so that you can communicate effectively with anyone in your life. "Relationship Resolution" provides tools to help you heal from narcissistic abuse by learning how to recognize gaslighting. This book will also help you understand abuse and control games in your relationships. It will teach you how to set boundaries, communicate effectively, and love yourself.

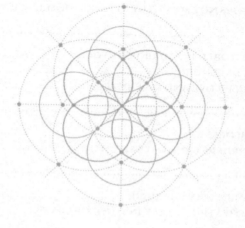

Healing quotes and daily journaling

Evette Rose

The healing intention of this book is to create awareness of your blocks and patterns. It is through awareness that healing, and transformation takes place. In this book you will find quotes and inspirations designed to heal and transform every day of the year.

Table of Contents

Getting started

Hi, my name is Evette Rose and welcome. I look forward to starting this journey with you to dive deep into challenges that you might be having in your life. Congratulations for taking active steps to improve your quality of life it takes courage to make a decision, but it takes determination to follow through on the decision that you made. Know that during this journey you are exactly where you need to be.

I invite you to move through this book with ease and with grace with an open mind.

I would love to stay in touch with you and you can join me on any of my events I always have weekly free master classes and free mini workshops.

You can join me on social media hang out have fun and enjoy a tremendous amount of free content that I also share.

Find me at: www.evetterose.com

Free MAT Membership site: www.matmembers.com

Free Masterclasses: www.matmasterclass.com

Introduction

Welcome to your self-esteem and self-love healing journey! I believe you are as excited as me to start this process and transformation. At least, I hope. Dealing with a pain point, such as self-esteem and self-love, can be a vulnerable process. I have been there, and I often linger in that pity party of feeling unworthy. It sucks. The emotions that stem from it can be strong and tremendously debilitating. It was for me, at least. Congratulations, because you finally took a step to give back to yourself.

This means that your journey of self-awareness, mindfulness, and your relationship with yourself is finally important enough for you to take action. As you know, if your relationship with yourself is not strong, it's going to be harder and take more energy to show up stronger and healthy for other people. It's also so much easier to give more to others than to give the same amount of love, understanding, and compassion to yourself. Imagine the amount of positive balance it would bring to your life.

It is important to ask yourself this question: "do I love myself enough?" Because you owe it to yourself. You have been your own companion through many challenges. You had lifted yourself up when other people failed to do so. You have leaned on your own through dark nights and hard mornings. You are the only person who has been and will be there for you through every second of this life until the very end. That relationship you have with yourself should be your biggest priority and investment.

Think of it this way: you are attending a pain-in-the-ass course, and you get to sit with someone you like. It makes it so much easier to bear through the lecture, instead of sitting with someone you dislike. If you cannot bear through a lecture with someone you don't like, how do you expect to bear through life with yourself if you lack self-love and self-esteem? With self-love comes self-confidence and self-esteem. It enables you to leave behind your fears and find positivity in this world. It allows you to have a more optimistic outlook, which lessens your chances of suffering from depression and unhappiness. It does not matter what anyone else in this world thinks of you, but what you think of yourself matters.

Those thoughts will determine what you can and cannot achieve in life. It defines who you are and can fuel your abilities to achieve whatever you want. It is very important that you recognize the amount of love you have for yourself. Recognition is the first and most important part of this journey. In order to start this journey, you need to know where you stand to prepare yourself accordingly for the path ahead of you.

This journey should be very near to your heart because if you look at your past, this will be the toughest journey for you to master, and while you haven't fully mastered it. It's still a journey for you, which is why the word journey is used here. Let's be honest. Life never stops being a journey. How we feel while we are on that journey will make or break our experiences.

In life, most things are not sprints. Life, healing, and just living your life, it's like a marathon. You pace yourself. Otherwise, you get exhausted. You get health problems, or you feel you can't do anything anymore.

When you run like a marathon, you run at your pace. Take your time because you're still moving, and you're not exhausting yourself. You have time to take in what is around. You have time to absorb your relationships. You practice self-observation as well throughout the process. It's easier when you don't feel you are always in a panic. There is power in calmness.

Therefore, you need to think of your journey of self-love and self-esteem as a marathon, too. You will run at your own pace and screw the voices on the side telling you what to do. You are probably feeling this way because you allowed too many of these voices to influence you. Well, I say enough with that. It's enough. There is no comparison, no standards, and no judgements. It is a journey you take for yourself and for your own good, and yes, I am here in the background supporting you, detached from your decisions and way forward.

You need to stop comparing yourself with others because you might be on the same sea, but you are in your own boat. There is no point in comparing yourself with anyone on this planet because there is only one person like you and that is you, yourself. Everyone has to master their own life on their own terms. Their purpose is not your purpose. If you keep comparing yourself with other people, you can never survive on the journey of self-love. You don't need to worry about other people's opinions, when it comes to self-love. Because no one is in your shoes; therefore no one gets to comment about the way you walk on the path of life.

Chapter 1

The journey

Why are self-love and your self-esteem important to you?

You just need to identify your "why." Why is self-love important to you? The answer to this question will be your motivation for the rest of the journey. It will act as an anchor and will keep you motivated through the hardships of the path ahead. Your purpose will help you commit to the journey of self-love.

Commitment is an essential item you need to pack with you if you plan to sail through the ocean of self-love. It will not come easy, but your 100% dedication will help you reach the shore. Let nothing become an obstacle in your journey. Your love for yourself matters, so you need to be committed to it. You need to make self-love a priority in your life, and then you have to treat it as a priority. There can be no excuses for loving yourself.

Another important factor that you should know on your journey of self-love is that self-love is not something that you can attain; rather, it is a practice and a conscious way of living that supports you to honor your true self and to make you feel good about yourself. Self-love is a practice of intentional acts to enhance our emotional, physical, spiritual, and mental well-being. Self-love is something that we owe ourselves.

Think of it as the unconditional love that a parent has for their child. If the child makes a mistake, the parent does not stop loving the child unless the parent is an ass, and yes, we have them. In most cases, the parent does not love the child less based on physical appearance or intellect. A parent does not hate a child for the grades they get at school. If a child is not good at sports, the parent would not hate the child.

They might disapprove, but not hate. In an ideal world, this is the unconditional love that a parent would have for a child. Self-love is about directing the same unconditional love toward yourself. Self-love is about practicing self-compassion regardless of your mistakes and imperfections. We deserve unconditional love, and we should not hesitate to give ourselves as much love as we need.

We should think of self-love as a sport. Being good at a sport is not something that you can gain in a day, but it is something that you need to work on. Just like a muscle that needs to be flexed, self-love needs to be learned in the same manner. Self-love needs practice.

There is a lot of scientific evidence that supports the notion of self-love. A lot of scientific evidence suggests that self-love can have a positive impact on your mental health, self-esteem, and your overall happiness. Society will continue to create a lot of pressure on us. We feel that we have a lot of goals to achieve, whether it is in terms of status and wealth or beauty. Sometimes it feels easier to focus on our failures, and we find it very difficult to look at places where we have grown. We keep striving for perfection, forgetting that humans can never be perfect. We forget to take care of our own basic needs, and somewhere along this journey, we then forget to love ourselves.

Some people view self-love as narcissism. But self-love has nothing to do with narcissism; it is not selfish. Working for self-betterment and taking care of yourself and your needs is not a selfish trait. We do not need to sacrifice our own needs for the happiness of other people. Self-love should not be defined as narcissism.

Self-love is a positive psychological practice, and it helps people to improve the general quality of their lives. It is not selfish to appreciate yourself for your growth. It is not selfish to care for your own self and to work for your betterment. Self-love has been scientifically proven to improve psychological functioning in humans. Some evidence-based benefits of self-love are higher self-high finish team, higher motivation, less anxiety, increased self-awareness, better sleep, and better mental health. Anyone can learn to develop self-love.

To develop self-love, it is essential to make space for self-reflection. In the modern world, we are running after materialistic gains. We have set a lot of standards for ourselves, and we are continuously working to meet those standards. In this race, we often forget to reflect on ourselves. If we do not constantly reflect on our own selves, then we become a stranger to our own selves. Self-reflection should be a ritual for us. A ritual is a practice in which we are mindful and aware of our intentions. There can be many ways of self-reflection.

It can take the form of journaling, a meeting with a trusted friend to talk about your recent experiences and challenges or reflecting on your life over a cup of coffee.

There are a few challenges you must face in order to gain self-love, but it is possible to overcome these challenges by avoiding self-criticism, adopting healthy rituals, having a safe environment, setting healthy boundaries, and appreciating the hard work we can gain self-love.

Neuroscience of self-love

Let us dive into the neuroscience of self-love. You might think that thoughts and moods are chemical reactions that take place in your brain, and you have no power over them. But modern science has proven beyond doubt you can change your thoughts and behavior, and it will rewire your neurological pathways and change the way you think. Therefore, it is very much possible for you to control the way you think. By changing the way, you think, you can change the way you feel and view yourself.

By rearranging your habits and optimizing your decision-making, you can harness your negative thoughts, become more centered, connected, and creative, and learn how to trust, prioritize, and love yourself. You can change your relationship with yourself by understanding how your brain works on a physical and chemical level and how it can be altered by changing behaviors, habits, and patterns of your thoughts. Love is considered among the top three behavioral motivations of humankind. Humankind is constantly obsessed with the idea of love.

When we fall in love, we feel all giddy, excited, and happy, not knowing if this is going to be wonderful or a heartbreak waiting to happen. This happens because when we fall in love, a lot of hormones stem from the brain. If we feel attracted to someone, our brain releases dopamine and serotonin. These are the happy hormones that make us feel excited and giddy. These hormones help us deal with anxiety and depression.

These hormones help us feel better. They even boost productivity. When we have more production of dopamine and serotonin, it helps us to sleep better, and it increases our appetite and digestion. Studies have also shown that the release of dopamine and serotonin increases our ability to learn and affects our memory. These hormones are associated with pleasurable sensations.

Dopamine and serotonin can act as the body's natural pain relievers. Psychological research shows that when we love ourselves and show care and compassion towards ourselves, a similar process takes place in the brain, meaning that the brain releases dopamine and serotonin. Self-compassion leads to motivation, optimism, and positivity. Studies show that when people are more compassionate and kinder towards themselves, they end up being more productive. When a brain releases dopamine, it literally changes the chemistry of the brain and helps us feel better. It starts with being kind and generous towards ourselves. Research proves that loving ourselves is scientifically good for our brains and body.

From the moment we are born until we die, love influences everything. It influences the decisions we make and the way we live. Art revolves around love. From our paintings to our writings, from our music to our calligraphy, love is everywhere. But we find it easier to love others than to love ourselves. Love for others comes more naturally than love for ourselves does. As if we were subconsciously programmed for self-criticism.

Research shows that 70% of the daily thoughts of a person are about criticizing their own self. We are often our worst critics. Even if we analyze our daily thoughts, it is evident that most of our thoughts revolve around criticizing our own selves, and we have very few positive thoughts about our own selves. Self-criticism is an evolutionary trait, although it helps us first with error correction and self-discovery. If it is hindering the amount of love, we have for ourselves, then this self-criticism should stop. Studies provide a very good evolutionary explanation for why we feel negative about our own selves.

Why is self-love so difficult?

Why does the love we have for others come so naturally? Even if we are aware of the advantages of self-love, it is something that we can't gain easily. It is a journey. It is something we need to work on. Little by little and day by day, loving others is something they teach us from the day we are born. We see people caring for us and loving us. It naturally makes us love and care for them back. We also love people because we do not want to lose them. This is not the case with our own selves. We are not afraid of losing ourselves the way we are afraid of losing others. The world constantly reminds us we need to love and care for others. But no one teaches us to love ourselves. It is something we must learn on our own. We are often reminded to do things for others but never for our own selves. We love people for who they are. But the problem here is that we don't know anyone completely.

We don't see other people's flaws that easily, as humans hide their imperfections. We love some people because we have to. We love other people because we like how we feel around them. We find it easier to accept other people with their imperfections, but we are hard on our own selves. We don't easily see beauty in our own imperfections. Therefore, we find it difficult to love our own selves. We see our flaws clearly and are more aware of our shortcomings than anyone else. We are the only ones who feel our emotions to their true extent.

When we are sad, we are the only ones who feel our pain. When we look in the mirror, we are the only ones who feel our insecurities. We think we are not enough. Not wise enough. Not beautiful enough. Not smart enough. Our minds are constantly echoing with negative thoughts about ourselves. Therefore, it becomes very easy to hate ourselves for the flaws we have but forgiving ourselves is where the beauty of our journey of self-love begins.

The moment we decide to forgive ourselves is the moment we lay the foundation of our ever-lasting love for ourselves. People who make us believe that the world was made only for them surround us and that their lives are perfect. We believe that the life they touched is better than the one we have. But the truth is that this life is a trial. We should not be fooled by what we see because it is only the tip of the iceberg.

We are unaware of whatever lies beneath the surface. Everyone has their own problems and their own demons to fight. If you find it difficult to understand, then you should ask yourself this question: "how well do you disguise your own demons?" Other people are doing the same. Life is not a bed of roses for anyone. Loving yourself does not mean that you need to accept all your flaws or that you need to like everything you do. Instead, it is the realization that you are capable of change. That you can do better for yourself. You can change yourself if you dislike who you are and create a better version of yourself. Self-love is about loving this transition and acknowledging your efforts to be who you are.

We are human beings, and we are supposed to experience a variety of emotions. It is ok to feel both kinds of emotions, whether they are positive or negative. Research shows that people who live wholeheartedly allow themselves to even feel vulnerable. Sometimes we can deny our uncomfortable feelings, ignore them, numb them, or try to talk them away. We can tell ourselves that we are being silly or that our emotions are not justified. But it is not possible for our emotions to just go away. If you do not acknowledge your emotions, then they appear in other forms.

We should think of our bodies as the physical carriers of our emotions, and if our emotions are not let out healthily, then they manifest themselves negatively in our bodies. It is very important to acknowledge our feelings and allow ourselves to feel whatever we are feeling. If we do not allow ourselves to express our emotions, then they bubble up inside us, and when they flow out, it is with such intensity that we cannot control them.

We should remind ourselves that we are not what we feel. We should remind ourselves that what actually represents us is how we deal with our emotions and bottle up our emotions. It's not a healthy way to deal with them. We should create a healthy and positive space for ourselves to express our feelings.

In the light of neuroscience, the reason we find it easier to focus on negative thoughts more is that the threat detection system of our brains stops in order to survive as a species. It is very important for our brains to detect threats and danger. Therefore, our brains have dedicated memory systems for storing threads and negative events, so that we can recognize endangering situations and prepare ourselves to deal with them.

But our brains do not have dedicated memory systems for positive thoughts. Therefore, it is very easy to remember negative thoughts as they are stored in separate sections in our brain, and it is very difficult to stick to the positive side. Negative thoughts are integrated with our brains immediately, but for positive thoughts to stick into our memories, we have to give them attention for about 10 seconds. Therefore, self-criticism is an evolutionary trait. It means that it is easier to remember negative feelings and stick to negative thoughts, but it also means that if we spend just 10 seconds thinking about something positive, then we can also keep that happy memory.

We should make it a habit that whenever we experience something positive or something we are grateful for, then we should dedicate ten seconds of our lives thinking about that moment so that it can stick in our memories. In this way, we can counter self-criticism with positivity. Self-criticism can lead to depression, eating disorders, and increased suicidal thoughts. In psychology, self-criticism is defined as a negative personality trait in which a person has a disrupted self-identity.

Self-criticism is the evaluation of one's own self. Self-criticism is often associated with major depressive disorders. People with better mental health are less critical of their own selves. Self-criticism is a rude, relentless inner voice that hurts us and does not make us feel any good.

It does not help us perform better at the moment, but we do not have to accept these negative thoughts about ourselves. A major goal of self-criticism is to silence our inner critic. Self-criticism often originates in our past relationships in our childhoods. Self-criticism can result from peer pressure at school, demanding teachers or bosses, strict parents, etc.

Self-criticism is a bitch, and it can also be developed from learned behaviors. No matter how you develop self-criticism, it can affect your mental health and well-being negatively. It hinders our opportunities because it fills us with self-doubt. It makes us believe we are not good enough and that we are not capable of personal growth.

Self-criticism does not define you. First, you need to believe that even if you think that your mind is programmed for self-loathing, you can change the way you think and develop self-compassion and empathy for your own selves. We should learn to love our own selves the way we love other people. We should show more compassion towards ourselves. We should make our minds a gentler space by thinking positively about ourselves. By being more aware of our feelings and taking charge of them, we can develop self-compassion. We need to remember that we are not our thoughts and that by taking charge of our thoughts, we can allow ourselves to feel less stressed and more at peace.

Chapter 2

Self-love does not mean the absence of self-criticism

The presence of self-criticism in a healthy amount is not bad. Criticism can also be constructive. It can be helpful, and it can help us improve our personal growth. Constructive criticism does not stand in your way when you try to improve yourself.

Therefore, we need to recognize ourselves and develop a healthy relationship with ourselves first.

We can use different ways to overcome self-criticism. Even if self-criticism is crucial for self-development, we need to silence this inner critic, and we need to stop thinking that self-criticism will motivate us to complete our tasks. No one is perfect in this world, so we need to let go of the idea of perfectionism, and we should enjoy making mistakes because we can learn from them. There can be different ways that we can use to overcome self-criticism.

The most important factor is to be mindful of our thoughts, feelings, and our reactions. It helps to create and keep a journal of your progress and read it whenever you feel you are not good enough. This will help you practice self-gratitude. You can also keep a list of your favorite personal qualities and the skills which you have.

You can get the help of your loved ones and your friends, as they can highlight some of your qualities that you are not aware of. Think of ways to be kinder to yourself. Start with small steps of kindness and acknowledge that your life will not change overnight, but by being kind to yourself, you can develop self-love.

We need to understand the process by which we understand ourselves and create an image of ourselves in our minds. When we meet another person, we gradually know them by analyzing their habits or by talking to them and by spending time with them. Our process of knowing our own selves is quite similar to knowing another person. We know ourselves because we spend a lot of time with ourselves. We know our experiences; we are aware of our thoughts in a way in which we cannot be aware of another person's thoughts.

The difference here is that what we know about other people is what they choose to show us about themselves; we cannot know another person completely. But when it comes to ourselves, we know what our negative thoughts are. Knowing our negative thoughts creates a sense of self-hate because we assume other people do not have such thoughts. The world leads us to believe that other people are perfect and that we are the ones at fault.

We are constantly defining our own selves. Even if we do not analyze how we react to different situations or what we think about different situations, unconsciously we are still using all this information to define ourselves. "The self" in the psychological perspective is defined as a mixture of conscious and unconscious thoughts and memories from experiences and future intentions; we create our own concept of "self." We do this through self-related processes.

These processes can help you observe yourself in the mirror and evaluate your personality. Our right hemisphere aids this process, which handles our ability to distinguish between ourselves and others. We mostly evaluate ourselves based on our experiences in life and how we react to different situations. During this process, we are fully aware of our thoughts, and it is easy to recognize the negative pattern in our thoughts.

Therefore, we can easily develop a feeling of self-hate for having these negative thoughts. We view other people as perfect because we are not aware of their negative thoughts as people are exceptionally good at hiding their negative parts. Self-love means being kind to one's own self in practicing the habit of self-compassion. This compression refers to being kind to yourself while knowing all your shortcomings and stopping yourself from destructive self-criticism. Self-compassion means treating yourself the same way you would treat a friend.

Modern studies have proven that self-compassion is related to better mental health and a lot of behavioral characteristics, such as positive body image. Self-compassion affects our mental health. By having compassion for ourselves, we develop better mental health, and it also improves our behavioral characteristics. If we have compassion for ourselves, we will refrain from negative thoughts on a daily basis. This process will help us develop better mental health. Better mental health leads to a better, happier, and more fulfilled life.

Therefore, it is very important to develop self-compassion. We may not be born with love and compassion for ourselves, but studies have shown that we can alter our neural pathways by changing the way we think about ourselves. So, by altering our thoughts, we can easily develop compassion and love for ourselves. The three underlying components of self-compassion are self-kindness, mindfulness, and common humanity.

We are used to blaming our own selves and judging ourselves harshly, but we should refrain from a critical analysis of our wrongdoings and our shortcomings whenever we have negative thoughts about ourselves.

We should replace it with kinder thoughts. It is ok to think that you can do better but we also need to remember that no one is perfect, and everyone has their shortcomings even if we are not aware of them. Self-kindness is a vital component of self-love. Be kind to yourself because you deserve to be treated with kindness.

The world is already harsh enough. We do not need to treat ourselves in the same manner. Although self-kindness does not mean justifying your wrongdoings, instead of self-kindness refers to acknowledging your beginnings, forgiving yourself, believing in yourself to do better in the future, and treating yourself with kindness. We are all humans, and no one is perfect. In fact, to be a human means to make mistakes. Self-compassion helps you to forgive yourself for the mistakes you make and move on from them so you can lead a happier life without your mistakes being a barrier to your happiness.

The journey of changing your neural pathways in such a way that helps you to lead a positive life begins by being motivated to change your brain and how you feel about yourself. Realizing that it is very important to rewire your brain in a way that is positive for you is the first and most wonderful step of this journey. It might be difficult, but it is not impossible. With a certain amount of reflection and self-awareness, we can rewire our brains to think more positively about ourselves. The journey can be very difficult, and for some people, it can even be uncomfortable. This is because the brain gets uncomfortable when we change its usual pathways.

Practicing something new means challenging old patterns of your neural pathways. Research in neuroscience has proven that when we practice new behaviors, skills, and new thoughts repeatedly, we can generate new and healthy neural pathways. By doing this, we can also change the default pattern of our thinking, and we can create a new default pattern for ourselves which benefits us in certain ways in which the old pattern failed. By changing our neural pathways from our default selves, we can create a sense of purpose and meaning in our life. We can make our relationships with other people more fulfilling and enriching. We can feel more productive, creative, and inspired. It can help us feel more present and more in control of our life, creating a sense of empowerment.

Self-love is tough. Let's be honest. It's so easy to give something to others that we cannot really give to ourselves at the end of the day. What that also does and what shows is a trigger of a lack of self-worth, feeling that we're not worthy of being as happy as other people. You are going to see how to find that and rediscover those parts and aspects of your sense of self again. Because it is there. It's just that there were perhaps moments in time, there were things that happened. There were maybe decisions that took place that blocked you from really stepping into this, from really embracing this beautiful relationship with yourself.

Recognize what is hindering you, so you can overcome it and develop a beautiful self-love relationship with yourself. Maybe you feel unforgiving towards yourself. Humans make mistakes. It is in their fundamental nature. None of us is perfect. But what matters is that you forgive yourself. You don't let it hinder your journey of self-love. You need to move on from your mistakes. Forgive yourself. You are worthy of your own forgiveness. Allow yourself to make mistakes because after all mistakes are what we learn from.

They are life's way of teaching us lessons. As we grow older, we feel that we are not allowed to make mistakes. We want to be perfect. But no such thing as a 'perfect human' exists. Making mistakes is acceptable. You do not need to be perfect. Make mistakes! Learn from them! And remember that our progress in life is not static. All of us are learning and growing. We are not our mistakes.

They are often the product of wounded thoughts and negative self-talk. It's not stemming from your core essence and soul of who you were before negative events. Therefore, you need to allow yourself to make mistakes and to learn from them. It does no good to dwell on mistakes. It only creates self-hate and hinders you from acquiring self-love.

We often think that in order to achieve success, we have to be competitive, and we have to constantly push ourselves. Research shows we are wrong here. Being self-critical and hard on ourselves is not a good thing. These factors are standing in our way to success. Scientific evidence suggests that self-criticism only makes us weaker, more emotional, and less likely to learn lessons from our failures.

Studies have proven that self-compassion is a better alternative to self-criticism. Self-compassion is not a weakness; it is a strength in the face of failure. Self-compassion gives us the ability to learn from our mistakes. It provides us with energy to try again with more enthusiasm this time. Self-compassion allows us to treat ourselves as we would treat a friend. It makes us more mindful of our needs and our feelings. When we can be gentler and more understanding of ourselves, then why should we be critical of ourselves?

When you look in the mirror, what do you see? Do you see yourself and smile? Do you find yourself beautiful? Or do you end up finding your flaws and trying to disguise them in ways that are uncomfortable for you?

An important factor that might hinder you from acquiring self-love may be your negative thoughts about the way you look. The way you look does not define your self-worth. Since the day we are born, feedback from our environment has conditioned us to believe that the way we look is of significant importance. What we need to tell ourselves is, "You are perfect just the way you are".

Your body is worthy of your affection. Beauty has no standards. A negative aspect of the world is that we have defined beauty in terms of standards set by people. But that is not the case.

Every person is beautiful. Every complexion in the world is mesmerizing. Every hair texture is a piece of art. And every face is itself the definition of beauty. You should not see your scars as imperfections, but as art that decorates your body in its own miraculous way.

Your body is worthy of your affection. It does so many things for you. It carries out so many functions that help you live your life. In return, it deserves to be loved and cherished by you. Instead of pointing out your flaws, count the blessings your body provides you with. Don't let some beauty standards on a piece of magazine fool you. You are a beautiful art that is worthy of nothing but love, praise, and affection. A simple principle you can adopt to help you cope with negative remarks from people is to know that what other people say about you comes from their own insecurities, and it has nothing to do with you. Don't let others define your worth. Honor your body. Wear what you want to wear.

Dress how you want to. Wear makeup if you feel like it, and don't if you feel more comfortable without it. Adorn your body the way you want to. Because that is what it is worthy of. The way you see yourself matters more than anyone else's opinion. If you are confident in how you look, it will reflect on the outside. You need to stop criticizing yourself. Only then you will be able to give your body the love and affection it is worthy of.

There will be days when it is very difficult to love yourself. Self-love does not mean that you have to love yourself all day and every day. It means that you have to be forgiving and soft towards yourself on days when you find it difficult to love yourself. Self-love is all about baby steps. There is no need to rush. You do not need to set any lofty goals for self-love. Because this is your own personal growth, and it has nothing to do with the world around you. This is where you get to be selfish and think only for yourself. You get to think for yourself and move at your own pace.

Self-love is sometimes confused with Narcissism, but there is a distinction between the two. Self-love is an act of self-compassion and self-empathy. In contrast, narcissism is a psychological disorder characterized by a lack of empathy for others and high regard for oneself. Narcissist people have an inflated sense of self-importance and a total lack of empathy for others. They have extremely fragile self-esteem and need constant reassurance from peers. Self-love is not narcissism, and there is a difference between the two. You can easily understand this difference by this example: if a narcissist achieves something, and no one is around to witness it, they don't even count it as success. But if a self-loving person achieves something, they don't need people to reassure them of their worth.

We spend more time with the world than we do with the world inside of us. Whereas it is very important to connect with our own selves, too. We are constantly running after materialistic gains in this world. We set one goal after the other for ourselves, and we are never done running. We do not look inside ourselves, and we are not aware of how we feel. All of it boils inside of us. Our unmet needs and our unfulfilled desires boil to the surface. But when it flows out, we are immersed so deeply in it we no longer have the power to understand it. At this point, we cannot understand what is causing us to react in the way we react. Therefore, we must consider it important to have a relationship with ourselves. And when we develop this relationship, we need to look after it and care for it just like we care for other relationships in our life.

Treat yourself with care. Do activities that restore your mental, physical and emotional well-being. Treating yourself or buying something for yourself should not be viewed as an act of materialism. Most acts of materialism have shown to negatively correlate with self-love and relate more to negative symptoms such as guilt.

Self-love is restraining yourself from things that will hurt you and caring enough about your own happiness to allow yourself to treat yourself occasionally. Think of it this way: self-left does not mean spending all of your salary on buying chocolates, but it means that you can buy yourself a bar of chocolate if you want to. Because negative thoughts stick in our brains, we need to remind ourselves continuously of the positivity in our lives.

By practicing self-care, we can give ourselves the message that we are worth the time, energy, and investment that we are making in ourselves when we do something self-soothing. It helps to calm down the limbic areas of our brain, which are activated because of stress and anxiety. If we are more aware of ourselves, we will know what makes us feel good, and it will be easy to calm down the limbic areas of our brain so that they do not activate stress and anxiety. It can help us feel calmer and more relaxed. We need to remember that life is what we make it. The way we think influences the life we lead.

If we think positively, there are more chances of us leading a positive life. It does not mean that we will not encounter any problems, but it means that we will have a healthier mindset to deal with these problems in a more positive manner. Our thoughts affect our perspectives, and our perspectives affect the life we lead. The amount of self-love you have for yourself will affect your whole life, so you need to work on it. It will affect your relationship with other people, and your progress ends your mental and physical health. You deserve to be treated with care, compassion, and love.

Self-compassion activates the self-soothing system in the prefrontal cortex inducing feelings of security, safeness, and attachment. Self-compassion deactivates the brain's thread system, which is in the amygdala and is associated with feelings of insecurity and defensiveness. Self-compassion results in a decreased level of stress. By developing self-compassion, people have reduced the number of stress hormones in response to acute stressors. This proves that self-compassion can actually change the way our brain works by altering our neural pathways. By changing the way, we think about ourselves, we can create positive thoughts and alter the way our brain works.

Just as there should be a balance in everything in our life, whether we relate it to spending money or giving time to our loved ones, there should also be a balance and the amount of kindness that we show others and ourselves. Research shows that when we show compassion to other people, it helps us lower our blood pressure, boosts our immune system and also helps us feel calmer.

They link these acts to primitive survival systems in our brain, which is wired to connect to and look after people as it helps us to survive as a species. Therefore, it feels so good to give compassion to other people. Still, we need to remember that giving compassion to ourselves is also important because if we do not have compassion for our own selves, we cannot give it to other people. If your cup is empty, you cannot pour water for other people to drink.

Our sense of self is very important in how we interact with the world and how we expect other people to treat us. By treating ourselves in a certain way, we teach others how to treat us. The diminished sense of self-worth can be an indicator of underlying symptoms such as insecurity, feeling of unworthiness in relationships, depression, anxiety, feelings of disconnection from ourselves, feeling of disconnection from others, and feeling lost in life. Self-love is a constant work in progress because it develops through different development stages of our lives.

As we grow older, we reach different levels of self-acceptance and compassion. By reaching deeper levels of self-acceptance, self-compassion, and self-love, we can improve ourselves and cultivate new and flourishing neural pathways that help us feel happier, worthy, and fulfilled.

Sometimes it is very important to analyze your environment and figure out who lifts you up and who drags you down. It is not possible to synchronize with the energy of every person in this world. Some people only drain us, and it is not selfish to let go of such people. In fact, it is essential to let go of these people if they do not take responsibility for their actions and do not improve their relationship with you. If you feel like someone is draining you, the first step should be to talk to them about it.

Tell them how they are affecting you and do it nicely. You should not be rude. Instead, talk to them and make them realize that their relationship with you is important enough for you to put effort into it. If you feel that these relationships are draining you even after all your efforts, then you need to let go of them. No matter how hard it is, take this step-in order to make your own life better. If you don't let go, you will only continue to hurt yourself, and hinder your journey of self-love because such relations will continuously pull you down instead of lifting you up. And you deserve more than this.

You deserve people who stand by you and help you develop a love like no other for yourself. You are worthy of such people. Anyone who drains your energy or pulls you down does not deserve your time and efforts. So, let go of them and do it for your own good. It might be painful but know that you are doing it for your own good.

Letting go of toxic people is even more difficult if it is someone you love. It will come with guilt and sadness. But there is no point in allowing people to drain you, because your love for yourself should be greater than your love for any other person on this planet. Your love for others should not keep you tied to a branch of thorns. You deserve the flower, not the pain. Love is not meant to hurt. It is meant to be comforting and beautiful. All relationships have their difficulties. But it is very important to recognize if a relationship is draining you, and if it is, then it's time to move on. It is important to put effort into relationships, but not at the cost of your own peace.

You do not depend on people for your happiness. You are enough for yourself. If you are in a relationship, it should be because you want to be in it. Not because you feel you need people around you to define your worth. You can live your life to the fullest. You should not need people to make you happy or define your worth. You can do that yourself. This is one of the toughest phases of the journey of self-love. It will take a lot of effort to realize that you can make yourself happy. But once you do, your love for yourself will increase, and you will also value yourself, just as you should.

Research shows that our brains are wired to be part of a supportive social network. It is our instinctive, primitive, and crucial need, and it helps us to survive and thrive as human beings. We cannot exist alone, nor can we flourish if we are around people who make us feel unsafe, exhausted, or judged. Research has proven that if we face social rejection, our brains experience it as a threat and emotional pain, just like actual physical pain is felt. So social support is important to emotional health and well-being. The relations we have with other people also help us define our self-worth.

Hence, it is very important to be surrounded by people who lift us up. It is important to be in an environment where we do not feel threatened, exhausted, or unsafe. Humans are very sensitive to their environment. Our brains need to feel a sense of safety and comfort, and peace in order to thrive. Research has shown that simple factors such as a plant in the room, natural lighting, soft textures, a scented candle, warm colors, pictures of loved ones on a wall, and some pinecones in a corner can help people feel calm and happy. So, it is very important to have a space where you feel safe and at peace. It is important to have such a space indoors and outdoors because it will help us feel safe and grounded.

Self-love begins the moment we decide to give importance to our own selves. The world constantly tries to make us feel we are not good enough, that we do not matter, or that we are not important enough. We feel as if the world is not giving us enough importance, so we stop giving ourselves importance, too.

It is very important to know our own selves and to give ourselves the importance of recognition we deserve. We should know what people or places make us feel uncomfortable or drained. We need to realize the external factors that make us feel peaceful. If we give information important to our feelings and give ourselves enough importance to consider how we feel in different situations and avoid situations that drain us, then we can give ourselves enough energy to do things that actually make us feel good.

Many people feel difficulty when saying no to something. Sometimes when we are asked favors, we feel it difficult to say no even if we feel drained or cannot fulfill the demands without causing harm to ourselves. But self-love means to put yourself above other people and their demands. It is ok to say no if we do not feel up to it. We should not burden ourselves to meet the demands of other people. Although self-love does not mean being selfish or not helping other people in need, it means putting yourself above the needs and demands of other people. Self-love is not the absence of empathy for other people, but a healthy amount of balance in empathy for yourself and other people.

The world is harsh enough, without us being harsh to ourselves too. We need to learn to treat ourselves with kindness. The world is full of harsh and hurtful words and critiques. So, we should at least speak to ourselves with kindness and love. We should show ourselves the love we expect the world to show us. We owe it to ourselves to be kind and loving to our own minds and bodies. It is ok to treat ourselves once in a while. We should celebrate our existence because it is no less than a miracle.

All of us have come so far from where we started, and we have grown so much. We are constantly trying to be a better version of ourselves, and this deserves recognition. We know how much we have suffered and how hard we had tried to lift ourselves up when the entire world was pushing us down, so we should be the ones who acknowledge our efforts, too. Don't wait for the world to tell you; you are worthy of love. Say it out loud to yourself.

To find joy within yourself, it is essential to find joy in the world around you. Look around you; it is a beautiful world. No matter where you are, I am sure you will find a lot of beautiful things around you. Make it a habit to notice the beauty of the world in which you live. By doing so, you will see the beauty inside yourself, too. Develop a habit of looking at the positive aspects of life more.

If you cannot find beauty, then create it. Buy a house plant, paint a wall in a color you like, or hang your favorite posters in your room, and change the world around you if the present one is not soothing to your eyes. It will help you find peace within yourself. Being in a better environment will help you flourish emotionally as well as physically.

A happy body and a happy mind will help you develop love toward yourself more easily. The environment has a significant effect on living things. Even a flower dies if you keep it in the dark. Work on creating an environment for yourself that does not hinder you from achieving self-love. This environment change should not only be restricted to our physical environment. We also need to let go of everything that is not serving us in the highest good. We need to let go of habits that do not benefit us.

First of all, we need to analyze which habits do not benefit us, and then we can replace these habits with better and more progressive ones. It is a slow procedure and will take time, but awareness is half the job done.

By being aware of which habit is not good for us, we are hallway on the road to letting go of such habits. We can start one by one and move on slowly, because as long as we are moving, the speed does not matter. Only the fact that we are moving on is enough. We also need to analyze which people are not good for us, and we need to let go of them.

The company we are surrounded with has a lot of effect on our emotional and mental health. If your company is draining for you, it is time for a change. You should not hesitate to let go of them. Surround yourself with people who love you, respect you, cherish you, and lift you up. If you are not surrounded by such people, then seek them and do not stop until you find what is best for you.

You can be your own best friend. You can talk to yourself. You do not depend on anyone. Treat yourself with love and kindness. Talk to yourself the way you would talk to a friend and be there for yourself just like you are there for people, because you deserve the best form of love, and that is self-love.

You need to love yourself. It is difficult, but you need to do it to acknowledge the beauty of the world, and to witness the beauty of every season. For dancing in the rain and playing in the sun. For chasing the butterflies and smelling the flowers. The trees stand tall through the winter, and so can you. The world is teaching you to be kind to yourself. Every caterpillar that turns into a magnificent butterfly teaches you that the process isn't easy, but the rewards are worth it. You need to love yourself so you can find beauty in the outside world.

So, you can feel the beauty of crisp spring mornings and the softness of the snowflakes that fall in winter. You need to love yourself in honor of the beauty of this world. We waste a lot of time by not taking ownership of our lives. It is essential to drop the victim mentality. Bad things happen to us, but it depends on what we do with them. We can use our pain as fuel to move forward. It is easier said than done. But it is possible, and it is for our own good. The moment we take ownership of our life, we feel in charge of it. This feeling helps in developing a love for ourselves. We take back control of our lives and move on with a renewed sense of hope and courage.

This power over ourselves helps us create change and move on from what drains us towards what lifts us up. By age four, our brain has developed 90% of its adult neural structures. By the time we turn this age, our templates for relationships and our core sense of self have developed. The right hemisphere of the cortex is highly active from birth till age 3.

This means that we are highly affected by non-verbal and sensory information at this time. Therefore, if we have a parent who is most well-functioning, relaxed, and self-giving and treats us with love, then we also learn to be self-giving. If we have a parent who has experienced trauma, is often stressed, depressed, anxious, angry, or does not treat us with love, then we also learn from their nonverbal cues that we are not good enough. It makes us feel we cause their stress or that we are overwhelming, or we are a burden to them. When our primary caregivers cannot meet our needs, then we might learn to get our needs met in ways that can be unhelpful later in our lives.

If our primary caregivers cannot provide us with a sense of security, then our perception of the world develops negatively, and we perceive the world as a dangerous place. It also affects our sense of self, and we view ourselves negatively. Our earliest relationships, therefore, affected our core sense of self. The way we feel our parents, or our caregivers view us highly affects our perception of our own selves. If our caregivers can provide us with the amount of love and care that we need, then we also view ourselves as delightful and lovable.

If our caregivers cannot provide us with this amount of love and care, then we view ourselves as unworthy of love, and it shapes a lifelong negative image of our own selves. Most of the people who face difficulty with self-compassion and self-love are people who have not been treated with love and kindness throughout their own childhood.

Although it is possible to change the way we think about ourselves, it is difficult if we have developed this image since childhood. As we grow older, our perception of ourselves continues to be shaped. We take all implicit and explicit cues that we receive from our environment, and we use them to shape our self-image. The queues that we use to shape our self-image are received from our parents, our teachers, our peers, our community, and also the media. The world made us believe that our worth is based on what we have or what we achieve compared to others. So, it has conditioned a lot of us to base our self-worth on external drivers and expectations rather than our own internal desires. From an early age, we view ourselves in the light of how other people view us.

We depend more on external cues than on our own abilities and self-worth. We feel we are not worthy of love because we were denied love at an early age. In most cases, we are not even denied love. What you may have needed from a parent was beyond their capacity to give you. If your mother or father never experienced love themselves, then their reference for love is wounded. Then you ask them to love you, and they misfire on this request because they don't know how. Imagine asking a street beggar if you can borrow $1000 from them. This same concept applies when you want love from a parent who is in a dire place of emotional lack.

We take a lot of time and effort to realize that how people treat us reflects their limitations and has nothing to do with our self-worth. The way our primary caretakers treated us was because of their own insecurities and difficulties. All of us are worthy of love. If they deny you care and love at an early age, it does not mean that you should deny yourself the pleasure of self-love throughout your life.

Chapter 3

Your inner world is a mirror of your past

Our self-image develops because of how people treated us when we were kids, but it is very difficult to trace this issue because we have a brief memory of that time. We had developed our self-image based on external cues that we received when we were not capable of retaining enough memory, so we are constantly in doubt about whether we were treated the way we thought we were treated.

That becomes your barometer of self-worth. It becomes your level of how you rate yourself in terms of what you are worthy of and what you're not worthy of. We view ourselves in the light of other people's opinions about ourselves. We develop a new perspective about ourselves, which is influenced by their thoughts about us.

We learn how to treat ourselves through other people. If people treat us right, we think we are worthy of it, and we treat ourselves in the same manner, but if other people treat us negatively, we assume we deserve it and our opinion about our own selves gets influenced by it. The important factor here is to know that this goes both ways.

We are aware of the symptoms, but we are less aware of the causes when it comes to developing our self-image. Even if it is hard to detect, it is very much possible to treat this issue because the brain is malleable.

By changing the way we think, we can change our neural pathways, as they are not set for life, and we can rewire them. This is not a straightforward task, because our default thinking has been establishing itself since our childhood. We feel, think, interact, and behave in a way that has been wired into our brains since we were little kids. We feel stuck in our feelings, and we feel it is very difficult to trace the origin of our emotions because they have been wired throughout our brains, and we are unaware of their origin.

Your journey with your relationship starts when you realize that a lot of your relationship dynamics with people in the past almost became like the mirror foundation of how you feel about yourself. It has a big impact in terms of how you feel, what you are worthy of, what you deserve in life, and what you can and cannot have.

This is one of the most important breakthroughs. You might have this with someone you cherish. It might be an enormous challenge for people to show up for you because they have their own demons to fight and their own destructive relationships to deal with. What might happen within that dynamic is that they might not give you the love, attention, and support that you so dearly need. It's not because they didn't want to.

I realized that the love I needed from certain people called them into a place and a vibration they couldn't relate to. They might not understand it. They might not even give it to themselves. And here you are, asking them to do something that they can't even give to themselves. Your need for love, which they couldn't give you, might have made them feel inadequate or shame. They might not understand these emotions in such detail. All they know is they feel uncomfortable.

So, let's switch gears for a minute. How do you feel when someone intentionally or unintentionally makes you feel awkward or shameful? Do you shy away and avoid them, or do you resist them by responding defensively?

A parent can respond either way as well when they are in a situation where you need them to show you emotions, they can't access themselves. Response from a parent will hurt. Either way, the result for the child is to feel rejected.

It's very common from a biological perspective to attack what we don't understand or to respond defensively when we feel awkward. How do you feel when you feel awkward? I know I feel vulnerable. It's normal to feel angry or defensive when we feel vulnerable. It's a safety mechanism.

We reject or push away what we mistrust or cannot understand. Most people don't remain curious to problem solve when they don't understand an emotional experience that took them beyond their capacity to interpret. Instead, things become a problem. They become a burden and then your attitude towards that shifts as well.

That is exactly what happens when you emotionally depend on someone. You will always receive the quality of emotional experiences that they can give according to their limits. So, what if their limits are then limiting you? Where do you draw the line? This is when self-love should kick in. With this awareness, you can change things around to be more balanced with your own emotional health and wellbeing.

Emotional dependency

There are very thin lines between gaining emotional support from someone and emotionally depending on someone. It's not always easy to recognize, but emotional dependence on other people is one of the greatest hurdles on the journey of self-love. Emotional dependence needs to be recognized in order to develop positivity in your life.

Experiencing anxiety and stress at the thought of being away from them. Not abandoning a relationship if it does not make you happy. Being submissive in a relationship. Not expressing your feelings, wants, and desires. Feeling inferior to your partner and not feeling good enough for them. Avoiding communicating your true feelings to avoid arguments. Always trying to please your partner, no matter how it affects you. These are symptoms of emotional dependence. It is no doubt one of the major advantages of relationships to have the provision of emotional support.

Your loved ones can show compassion and comfort while you are under stress or adversity by listening to your problems and validating your feelings. You might go to your spouse first in a romantic relationship if you need this support. It's common to want emotional support and direction from partners, especially in committed relationships.

There is no harm in seeking comfort from loved ones in times of need. But emotional dependency goes beyond the point of emotional support. Most romantic couples rely on one another to some degree.

However, you're probably not doing much to address those needs on your own when you depend entirely on your partner to do so. Your relationship and general well-being may eventually suffer from this complete reliance on another person because it is a harsh reality that the only person who can always be with you is yourself. No matter how much you love someone or how much they love you, it is impractical to think that they will always be with you. Therefore, relying on someone to the extent of emotional attachment is not a good idea.

Emotional dependence does not lead to healthy relations. You are constantly in need of reassurance, which can drain the other person. Emotional dependence is a hurdle to both your relationship with your partner and with yourself, too. You should be comfortable with your emotions, and you need to be in charge of them. You are the master of your own sea. People can support and be there for you through your journey, but you have to be in charge of your own happiness, as no one else can do this for you beyond a certain point.

The more you need love, the more inadequate the person you depend on will feel, and the more it stirs up anger in them. The more they will feel that you are the source of their inadequacy. And, of course, they will attack you because they subconsciously associate you with feeling that inadequacy, which will trigger their low self-esteem. Feeling unable to be there for you, feeling unable to love and connect as well as be around you in your time of need.

Defining self-love and self-esteem.

Self-love is often defined as having an awareness of your well-being and happiness. This definition is a little too short. It cuts out so many other important factors that also need to be kept in mind when you explore such a deep topic, especially when you start a self-love healing journey.

Together, we are going to be exploring steps, different concepts, and challenges behind self-love. Ultimately, we'll go through it step-by-step and break it down.

Let's define what your definition of self-love is. Here's the reason this is important. If your definition of self-love is wounded or traumatized, then your definition might be built on a vulnerable foundation.

Your definition of self-love sets forth what you feel you can and cannot have. That's where your limitations can start. But that's also where you can break down these limitations easily. Sometimes our definition of self-love is also what we think it should be by looking at what other people are doing, what mentors are saying, what teachers are saying. We failed to recognize that the definition of self-love is all about what feels right. What do you feel you need in order for you to know and understand that you are loving yourself right now?

What does self-love look like? What does it mean? How would you like to feel in a relationship with yourself when you are loving yourself? Take a moment and think about it.

What is your definition of love? What is it? How do you know you love yourself if someone had to ask you? Pretend that you are actually explaining this now to someone, and hopefully that might also help you find a much better way to explain this and express this, but expressing this also towards you.

What is your definition of love?

_____

What are your self-love values?

Let's also define what your values for self-love are. You can establish what self-love is, meaning your values behind it by writing ten values. There should be ten points that start with: "I know I love myself when I'm feeling, seeing, sensing, or doing _____." Write them down from most important to least important. Please write ten.

This is a great exercise because now, when you look at these values, especially the highest, it might be something you feel is very important to you.

We're going to be diving into quite a lot of concepts and also signs of self-love. We will also look at the underlying root causes why we have these signs and symptoms.

Chapter 4

Self-love blocks

Let's look at the first sign of self-love challenges. One of the many common ones is worrying about what others think about you. This is a very common, deep-seated, hidden worry that most of us can relate to. Ultimately, we're always looking at others to either validate what we do or say.

We often use people's reactions towards us as a reference, almost like a barometer, for understanding where we are connecting with them, or maybe when we cannot do so.

We also lose tremendous power when we judge our worth based on feedback from people. Your power is not with you in this case. It means that people can make or break your self-esteem based on their judgments, verbal communication, projections, and feedback. You also should remember that people can only take in and observe aspects of you based on what their mindset and emotional state are, allowing them to observe through their own limited filters.

Remember that you filter in what you energize. The same applies to others. If they are in a negative place in their life, then they might only see and focus on your mistakes. They can't see beyond that. That is not your problem. They cannot observe what is good about you.

Another way of explaining this is to remember when you are having a bad day. All that you see around yourself feels negative. Suddenly, you focus on people's poor qualities as well. It's challenging not to feel disconnected from people when they judge us.

Have you noticed that you often judge your self-worth by how connected you feel to people? But what if there is a disconnection because they can't feel the love themselves? You then, without conscious thought, assume it's because you are not good enough. Let that sink in.

Another aspect and symptom of lack of self-love is feeling guilty about doing things on your own and for yourself. This was a very strong pattern for me. This stems from always wanting to make sure as a child that your parents are happy, and you do what they want you to do. That emotional reward might have made you feel as if they see, hear, and acknowledge you. Being human, we want rewards for our actions. It is very common to do stuff for others, as it feels more rewarding.

When we do something for others, we like the attention we get. When we do something for ourselves, there is no feedback or immediate validation. You didn't feel that same amount of acceptance. Losing attention, acceptance, or the absence of it made you feel unworthy. It might have made you feel you can't do what you want because you didn't have that emotional reward following your action.

We often end up feeling selfish after we do something for ourselves. Even if you analyze your routine, how many things are there that you do for yourself and yourself only? There are hardly a few things, apart from basic survival habits, that we do for ourselves.

Apart from that, having to achieve a goal and not feeling worthy enough to accomplish it on your own and perhaps not having support or guidance to complete it. That also plays a big role in feeling confident about doing what you want to do.

You know the feeling when you're doing something, and you make a mistake? Then your parents, or someone, says, "I told you so." It's upsetting. Surely you can relate. So, what happens? If you want to do something again, you're going to feel guilty about not having listened to someone or not taking someone's advice.

This creates a very lasting impact on your self-confidence. You believe you are not good enough to achieve things. You compare yourself to others, and you spend so much time doubting your skills and abilities that you barely have time for the task itself. Accomplishing a task requires you to believe that you can do it first. If you think you can, then surely you can. It is all about mindset. You can accomplish as much as you think you can. Having been told as a child that you cannot accomplish something can create a voice in your mind. This voice constantly keeps telling you, you are not good enough. Self-love is the voice you can use to respond to this negative voice and tell it, " I am capable."

We live in a fast-paced world where we develop a habit of wanting instant gratification. We want results as soon as we start a task. But some tasks are hard to accomplish and require us to try again and again. This creates frustration, and we believe we are not capable enough of completing the task. This results in a feeling of self-worthlessness and hinders our journey to self-love.

In most cases, this stems from feeling unworthy, and doing what you want. The result? Your needs are not met. When you perhaps did that in the past, and it created some level of some discomfort for someone else, or maybe a parent made you feel guilty for not doing something that they wanted you to do, so your emotional reward is normally about the parent and not about you. This can become a toxic cycle, which leaves you chasing after other people's needs.

Another one is the on-and-off struggle with eating disorders. I often noticed that this is an enormous problem. People who feel out of control in their life due to pressure, perfectionism, and feeling controlled in their life struggle with self-love challenges.

Control is being exercised by knowing what a person can and cannot eat. Also, even just the resistance to eating something that a person knows they would really love feels empowering. This is often motivated by feeling out of control in one's life. There is overcompensation for trying to gain control by controlling something they can, which is their diet.

When you don't eat for a while, your body gets used to it. It gets used to not receiving a certain amount of food, and the hunger pains will then go away.

That feeling of neutralism in your stomach gave you a sense of empowerment and accomplishment. The need for control is mastered, and the satisfaction of feeling you are in control becomes so significant that you continue to repeat the cycle of not eating. This can become dangerous as eating disorders can start this way.

Eating disorders can also switch

It also depends on your emotional state because when you are feeling unhappy, food can also become comforting. In most cases, food can be a person's comfort because it is safe. It doesn't talk back to you. It makes you feel good temporarily.

We also perhaps want to look and feel good. Social media is trashed with these unrealistic body types and shapes, which in most cases, comes through filters and just standing in the right position. It is not even real, yet we try to live up to it.

We try to become something that is not even real. We try to push and force our bodies to become something that is almost unnatural.

The result? Pain, because now we go against what our natural body shapes are and the functioning of it. Not only are you creating an emotional and psychological conflict within yourself, but you're also creating conflict with your biological body which is also connected to your appetite, and whether you feel safe or unsafe.

When you are in a state of distress, it often can trigger a need to eat more because the body is burning a lot of energy to stay in a fight-or-flight state response. What can also happen is that when you are in a state of distress, you freeze or hide. There are people who feel safe and happy by eating more.

The reason for this is their body is relaxed, and it's able to focus its attention on what it needs. In this case, feeling our emotions by itself is not safe. We control our emotions by engaging in an activity to stir up feelings in a controlled way.

We also have what is called comfort eating because of emotional associations that have connected to food and lacking these emotional resources within ourselves as well. We try to connect to these emotions through food.

Another symptom is giving too much of our time and energy to others. This is something all of us can relate to. Or at least there must have been phases you went through.

Just a question for you.

Have you noticed what you do the most for others is perhaps what you desire the most? You might feel so unworthy and too uncertain to take action and do more of what you need the most for yourself. Instead, we live our lives and happiness through other people.

Another symptom is always apologizing for mistakes that we make or apologizing for something that is not even our fault. Can you relate?

This pattern stems from feeling unworthy of just basically existing. That feeling like everything is your fault. This comes from a deep fear of being judged. Maybe you were judged countless times. You are perhaps punished a lot. There might be a part of you now expecting to be punished or wronged. It's just lingering there in the back of your mind. Maybe people who couldn't take responsibility for their actions and used you as the scapegoat. The reasons could be endless.

Sometimes we also apologize in advance before something even goes wrong. This is when a part of you is expecting to do something wrong. You constantly think that it doesn't matter what I do; I'm going to do it wrong. This often also comes from an upbringing where a parent could have been very critical.

Another symptom that we have is you might have felt that your personality in public is fake, and you can't just be yourself. It's also known as the imposter syndrome. You always feel like a fraud. Even when you are smiling, deep down, you are hurting so much, but you refuse to show your discomfort.

If you allow someone to see your vulnerability, there's a fear of being ridiculed. There's a fear of being humiliated and being judged. This stems from not being able to voice and express yourself when you need to throughout your life.

Then having to act and behave in ways that make other people feel happy because if you can make them happy, it means that you are important to them. You feel validated. You're getting attention, you're getting love, and you're getting your needs met. The result? You are becoming something that you're not without even realizing it. Whereas, if you felt you matter, then this would not be an issue because you would already be authentic and buy into people's drama and shortcomings.

I know it's easier said than done. It is hard to practice. Especially if it has become a subconscious part of your lifestyle. It's not just changing your personality; it's also changing your behavior and lifestyle. A lifestyle that you have built around yourself and a personality that does not align with who you truly are.

If you're going to step into a role and behave in a certain way that other people approve of, then you're moving further and further away from who you really truly are. You're going to feel like a fraud because you can't connect and relate to yourself. It's not that you are a fraud; it's because of the disconnect that you feel within yourself.

In short, the reason for this is that you're trying to connect to your true identity in the background. You have an awareness of it, but you don't know how to allow that part to be revealed. The result? Your authentic identity is unsafe. It feels unsafe to be heard and seen. When we create these false identities, which of course, now feel foreign, the more you feel like a fraud, the more your relationship and the more your body is asking you to come back.

Another symptom is that you have a strict perfectionist routine. You might feel the other extreme of not just caring anymore, such as feeling passive. You may even go through both cycles. Because of exhaustion of the extreme polarities, you might overcompensate because you feel burnt out from always having to have everything perfect. This pattern also stems from needing to control everything in you.

By being a perfectionist, at least you can control certain aspects of your life.

At the end of the day, what a perfectionist is seeking is to just emotionally, and psychologically feel safe and accepted. To feel secure within their dynamics, within themselves and also other people. This association of being perfect = being in control, is an unhealthy pattern. A person can become used to this pattern. To feel in control, they always have to be perfect. So, it's a Catch-22. When you feel you have to have everything perfect, you put so much pressure on yourself and feel all these burdens emotionally and psychologically.

It turns and becomes a very vicious cycle that feeds into itself. It's just a matter of time before you develop more coping mechanisms to cope and to deal with stress that is stemming from this toxic pattern. This is almost like the start of a negative cycle that most people can have. This can also feed into eating disorders.

Another symptom is that your relationship with yourself becomes a mirror and a reflection of how you were treated in the past. We have covered this before. We measure our self-worth and value based on how people treated us in the past. The more love you receive, the stronger your confidence is within yourself. The stronger your self-worth will also be. The clearer your sense of clarity within your identity would be. Why? Because your identity feels accepted, seen, and acknowledged. If this flips to the opposite, then it will have a big effect on your confidence and how you feel about yourself.

It does not at all mean that it's your fault for allowing people to mistreat you. In most cases, this could have happened at a very early age in your life, which means you didn't really have a lot of control over how you were loved or treated.

What is important to know is that the more you were interacted with in positive ways, such as, eye contact, communication, and physical touch, the more your limbic system, (hippocampus, your emotional brain) would have been stimulated resulting in a very healthy development of the emotional brain.

This part of the brain also holds long-term memories. It is also in this part of the brain that we can develop neurogenesis and neuroplasticity, which means the part where EPF in hormones is released. It can cause new neural pathways to grow, and also, for existing pathways to change, to strengthen, or become weakened, which is known as neuroplasticity.

When your emotional brain has not been stimulated in a healthy way during your childhood, these sections can actually become under-stimulated. What would that look like? Well, social anxiety, shyness, avoiding communication with others, struggling to physically interact with people (hugging someone, holding someone's hand), or being physically close to someone else.

The beauty of the brain is that we can stimulate the emotional brain again and heal from the absence of positive stimulation (interaction) during our childhood.

How you communicate with yourself, meaning your inner dialogue, is also very important. Communicating with yourself is as important as communicating with other people is. Our inner voice is constantly talking to us. From the second we wake up to the moment we fall asleep. We need to talk to ourselves nicely. There is no harm in addressing yourself with as much love as you address others with.

The importance of speaking with yourself kindly can be clear from the fact that in the Solomon Islands, when people need to cut a tree, they don't actually cut it. They curse it daily. They scream and shout at it, and eventually, it dries and dies. This is the same case for talking to yourself. The way your inner voice treats you is important for your well-being. It should be filled with love and care. If you don't treat yourself with kindness, the world will do the same. Remember that what you feel about yourself reflects your subconscious mind.

Let us realize that this deep internal expression reflects someone else's emotional unavailability that was projected onto you.

Let's continue to talk about more symptoms of self-love and dive much deeper into these concepts. The more you understand why you feel the way you do, is called awareness. Awareness of a problem is a problem half-solved. The other half is healing tools that you apply to your life.

Another part that I want to discuss is self-awareness equals self-love. Even if you have that awareness, do you know what you need and what you should give to yourself? How do you know If you don't have full awareness of what your needs are in the first place?

How do you know when you are overstepping your own emotional and physical thresholds and boundaries? Something to think about.

That brings me to another form of self-love: to love yourself enough to know and understand where your limitations, thresholds, and boundary limits are. If you don't have an awareness of how you want to be treated, then how can you attract the right partner, friendships and dynamics, and even communicate it?

Awareness of oneself leads to an awareness of emotions. It is very important to be aware of the emotions we feel and to embrace them openly. All emotions are human, and it is ok to feel every emotion, whether it is happiness or sadness. You are allowed to feel every emotion at its full intensity.

Loving yourself does not mean that you will not feel negative emotions. It means allowing yourself to feel whatever you feel. With self-love comes self-awareness. Both concepts go hand in hand. Loving yourself enables you to know yourself enough to recognize your emotions.

You can dive into your sadness and dance in your happiness; the world cannot stop you from doing so. Loving yourself means giving yourself permission to feel whatever you want to feel and not limiting yourself or your emotions. You can embrace your emotions in front of people you love, and you don't have to bottle up your negative emotions only for them to flow out with such intensity that you cannot control them. If you allow yourself to embrace your emotions, you stay calm like a water bottle, which remains calm even when it is shaken. But limiting your emotions and not allowing yourself to express or feel them is like shaking a soda bottle violently and then opening it.

In most cases, you might have wanted things in relationships that's based on lack, meaning you wanted people and objects from the outer world to fill an empty inner world. If you don't have an awareness of your level and your barometer of self-worth and also your value, then how can you act in ways that would show self-respect?

Awareness of your inner world is key. If you want to change your inner world, then note. Your inner world is consistently being shown to you in your relationships, dynamics, and how unhealthy your relationships are.

That also includes yourself. How should you avoid letting old emotions about yourself recycle themselves? It's realizing them and becoming aware of them as they arise, and then letting them be there. Let them be there without that messed up toxic judgment. They're there for a reason, for them to be explored and be released. You want to be free from feeling this discomfort, right?

The part of you that holds the most pain is the part that needs the most love. That pain comes from maybe not feeling adequate enough to address, resolve, or heal it. It's through understanding and self-awareness that we build self-compassion. That is how we start the healing process of valuing what is important.

There's also more to self-love, and that is compassion. Here, compassion for yourself, such as self-compassion, is part of the expression of self-love. Showing love and compassion towards yourself is not victimhood. It means that you recognize your need for comfort, love, and self-care during these challenging times.

Chapter 5

When you are pushing up creek

As we know, it is easy to always be in the flow, loving, and connected to yourself when things are going well. It's also when things go bad that we feel more challenged to love ourselves and to be there for ourselves.

Challenging times might have made you feel really isolated in the past, which caused you to feel very disconnected in your relationship with yourself and feel that you cannot fully fulfill your needs on your own. Perhaps making you feel you don't have what it takes to be there for yourself. As a result, you might look for support, reassurance, and love outside of you. Now at an outrageous price, your self-esteem will determine the support you feel you are worthy of.

In most cases, the result of what you get instead of what you want will not be as positive and as empowering as you need to be. Self-love and self-compassion are often mistaken for weakness and self-love can also be experienced as a form of cowardness. As a society, we've also abused ourselves with hardworking hours, cutting ourselves off from necessities and trying to find success through suffering.

In most cases, we were also taught that success doesn't just come easy and you have to suffer before you can achieve success. There's no space for self-love and self-compassion in suffering. It can also make a person feel they are weakening their mindset, lessening their chances of actually achieving success if they showed themselves self-love. It's hard to show self-love when you are in a state of lack, desperation, and competition. It's a completely different frequency match.

Are you motivated by lack instead of love?

We are perhaps even motivated by pain and not by love. Lack motivates us as we try to counterbalance it instead of feeling motivated by love. We act when we are desperate, and we act when our most basic needs are not stable or being met. We can even associate our success with negativity, just as we associate success with suffering. If we switch gears and move away from negativity and suffering, we might lose what we have created through these challenging thoughts and mindsets.

Self-love is such a weakness in society. It's judged. It's laughed at. Sometimes social acceptance is more important than a healthy relationship with ourselves. If we had it, we would not have cared about social acceptance. It's because we don't know what self-love looks like and how it will feel when we make it to the other side that causes blocks in trying to achieve it.

Self-love improves your performance skills, believe it or not, instead of your confidence being driven by lack or fear of loss, or maybe fear of being humiliated, which can now also lead to poor decision-making because you're acting from an impulsive state of mind. When you make a decision based on fear, how you think, feel, and interpret information is greatly influenced by pain, and past traumas, which are now clouding your judgment to make a sound, solid decision.

When you make a decision and act from a place of self-love, it means that you are acting from a place of healthy confidence and healthy reassurance that you can create what you want with ease and grace.

Acting from a place of pain means all trauma wounds would deplete your energy levels because your stress hormones are activated, and you become reliant on adrenaline that's being released to act. As a result, you associate your success with this adrenaline and stress. This hormonal stress response keeps you in a negative state of mind because the subconscious mind is now searching and on the lookout for a potential threat, which it is expecting. What exactly is it expecting?

Judgment and lack. That threat is a lack, but the lack is in your mind. This pattern now becomes like a broken record that keeps playing, but only to the detriment of your happiness, health, and your relationship with yourself.

Here's something else we will discuss, and that is the power of shame and guilt. Let me introduce shame and address the challenge with this in relation to self-love. As a starting point, let's first explore the good side of shame before we tackle it as a negative experience in our life.

Sometimes shame serves you positively in life, almost like a humble reminder when the ego has spiraled out of control or when you're being ungrateful in moments when appreciation should be embraced.

Feeling shame is a part of you that recognizes your behavior or has now become out of alignment with who you are. Shame serves as a wakeup call when you're wrongfully hurting someone else. The shame is there to show you to correct your behavior and correct a situation where you may have been the source and the cause of someone else's pain and hurt.

Shame also spirals out of control to a point where this gentle reminder has now become very toxic in many other areas of our lives.

This also stems from always feeling responsible for the needs of other people, because when we handle the needs and the happiness of others, then deep down, this ensures that our dynamics with them remain safe. Our connection with them also stays strong, even if you are unhappy in that dynamic. It ensures that you will not be abandoned or rejected. In a subtle way, you also feel in control of the dynamic because you serve a purpose within that dynamic. For example, when they're happy and they feel taken care of, it keeps the peace to a certain degree.

We also establish our self-worth by how much we sacrifice our value. We have a purpose that stems from how much we can contribute to the quality of life of someone else. This is quite a beautiful concept. However, this approach can also require an equal exchange, and the lack of this exchange can make a dynamic very unhealthy to where you give too much and neglect yourself. This is called self-abuse. It's when your relationship with yourself takes a toll on your awareness of your health and your emotional needs and physical needs.

Your childhood also plays an enormous role and relationships that maybe you had with partners also contribute.

We also have another factor coming into play, and this is a little more out of our control. That is the influence of society. People starve and neglect their true, real, and genuine needs in order to come across or be seen in a certain way. Beauty, money, and extravagant living have now taken the lead in many areas and parts of our lives and, frankly, are accepted by society.

It's popular. It's cool. It's great. Well, what we're saying deep down is the root cause that it's cool to suffer.

But we do it anyway. It's cool to destroy your identity and your sense of self. That's actually what's happening.

All this is for the price to be accepted, feel included, and avoid isolation. Isolation is not in our true nature. Genetically, we're designed to live in communities the same way our ancestors did. The price that we are paying to avoid this forever-growing isolation cycle and this life has now become really toxic to our health. It's become unhealthy for our relationships with ourselves. Especially how much we value our identity, who we are, what we are, and what we contribute. So much energy is invested in doing more.

We now ensure our value, worth, and sense of purpose. However, it is also through needing acceptance that we cannot accept ourselves because of our investment in someone else's life.

This frustrating part is that you will always have to work for love and acceptance in order to feel fulfilled within yourself. The reason for this is that your sense of acceptance is reliant on reactions and behaviors from people in your outer world. You will now rely on your environment to make you feel a certain way. The downside to this is that your environment always changes.

Your dynamics with people will always change. That means that everything that you rely on in order to feel a certain way can change at any given time. That means that your relationship with yourself and the stability of that is now in the hands of your outer world.

Self-love is a divine dance, almost like a dance between femininity and masculinity. We always have this idea that women should be feminine, and men should be masculine. But how does that fall into place with self-love?

In society, we deem this as wrong. It's not acceptable. What is a masculine man supposed to be like and feel like? A man is a human being, having a human experience. What that looks like is every person's choice. Who is now to say what a man should look like, what they should dress like, and what they should behave like? It's just old traditions. It's society and its expectations. These traditions give us a sense of safety and stability because it gives certainty.

The flip side of this is also the same for women. What if a woman does not resonate and relate to being feminine? Their personality and who they are might be more masculine. In society, we deem this as wrong or not acceptable. It's not acceptable. Women and men are also looking for healing, work around, healing these aspects of their identity that they once felt uncomfortable with.

People are now being told how they should feel and behave and if your femininity or masculinity does not cause you to feel discomfort, if it does not influence your quality of life, why fix it? Why are you creating a problem where there is no problem? Confused? Perfect. You are exactly where you need to be. You see, self-love is a gentle femininity that we all have. Regardless of whether you are a man or woman, this beautiful balance between masculinity and femininity exists in everyone. Our associations and definitions of these inner aspects of ourselves greatly sabotage and even destroy our ability to connect, express, and honor it. Through this inner balance we tap into self-love into self-compassion because self-love is also now an equal approach to masculinity and femininity within that.

This also includes the art of knowing when to step into your masculinity and when to step into your femininity. For example, when I look at myself and my patterns, I step into my masculinity when I have to assert boundaries, which, for me, is self-love. For me, it means that I'm respecting myself. I'm respecting my threshold and my limitations. When I teach, and I step into my femininity as the energy flows better when I need to connect to my intuition and perhaps give compassion and advice. This allows me to have an awareness of my needs in a self-compassionate way throughout the day.

Femininity and masculinity are back-and-forth dances in everyday life. My conclusion to this is that you should love yourself enough to embrace whichever side of the fence you are dancing on and allow yourself to be dancing on both sides.

Chapter 6

Let's do something really fun. We are going to test what some of your resistances are towards receiving love from yourself. We are going to observe how your emotional body respond to these questions.

What are your associations with self-love?

How do you react to it?

How do you feel about it?

So, I am going to take you through a really powerful exercise here through our healing meditation to connect to these parts and aspects of this.

This is just a fun test. This is just to get a feel for where you are at in terms of giving love to yourself, and then closer to the end of this activity, we're going to be testing it again by reevaluating.

What is happening to your healing journey from this perspective?

We're going to be diving into the subconscious part of you that might reject that part of you that loves you. We're going to unravel it, see where the challenges are, and see what the blocks are, but in a very fun and easy way.

The intention here is to give your subconscious mind a voice, to see the hidden messages in your body that we might have been perhaps avoiding or not observing in the way we should be.

The self-love stepping exercise

For this exercise, I invite you to pretend that you are happy. You are going to imagine a version for you that is 100% confident and filled with self-love in life. So, what you'll do is to stand up with an open space of at least two meters or six feet in front of you.

At the end of these two meters or six feet, you are now going to pretend that you can either hear, feel, see, or sense a copy of you that is 100% confident and filled with self-love in life.

What would you look like?

What would you feel like?

What would you sound like if you really truly had healthy self-esteem and loved yourself?

What would it feel like if you had all your needs met?

Now, slowly, slowly, slowly, walk towards that part of you. As slowly as possible, and you're going to feel emotions coming up. If you feel frozen, step into that feeling. Continue to step into whichever emotion arises until you get to the end. Until you reach the happy version of yourself. Once you do, step into that version of yourself and merge with it.

This process is going to reveal many aspects of yourself. I would highly recommend that you journal your experience when you are done. I have very important questions to ask you once you are done with your exercise.

Question 1: What were your five most dominant reactions during the exercise?

Question 2: What do you need to let go of in order to become fully happy?

Question 3: What do you need to accept about yourself so that your light can shine?

What are you going to do with the answers to these questions? Knowledge is power, but that power is useless if it's not acted on. The ball is now in your court.

If you feel a block, then you can always head over to my recorded session www.guidedhealingsession.com which is in our free MAT Membership site under courses.

Chapter 7

How do you know if you love yourself?

After playing and after having fun, after working through some breath work and also meditations and positive affirmations, and also diving deep into the subconscious mind, we will see how you are feeling now.

We are going to start off by observing how your self -love values perhaps shifted or changed.

Here's the thing, they don't have to change. But it's interesting to see that if we heal, our values can actually change. The more awareness you have of these values, the more you can consciously align yourself with people, activities, and actions that can bring more awareness regarding self-love into your life.

When you are ready, write ten values for most important to least important once again. For example, I know that I'm loving myself when I do something, or when I take certain actions, when I feel certain feelings, or when I hear certain things. Write ten, and then once you've written them down, look at your list that you wrote earlier and see how they have changed (if they did).

How did you go? Did you find any changes? Did you find anything that could have been different, something that shifted,?

Did the highest value that you have from the last exercise change or has something else perhaps come up?

This is a really beautiful journey, and these values will continue to change. However, it's important to build mindfulness and awareness around what these values are. Because the more conscious you are aware of it, the more you can align yourself with it.

Now we will move on to the next exercise. We are going to do the self-love healing test. Here we are going to see how much you have shifted, to allow yourself to love yourself by just having more awareness. We're going to be doing the self-love exercise again.

Also remember that now when we do this exercise, if you feel you have made as little progress as you would've liked to, remember, they did not build Rome in one day.

I invite you now to reconnect with a sense of belonging and a sense of purpose, and also a sense of just loving yourself while you can also do something for someone else.

When you are ready, take your computer, or pen of paper, and answer this question.

Rate how you feel now out of ten. Ten being happy and content with yourself, and zero is being completely and utterly unhappy.

Once you've done that, write the answer to this question.

Think back to the times when you helped someone else to have courage in their life, maybe supported someone through a hard time, maybe someone who was sad, or someone who was feeling down. I would love for you to write whatever you did or gave to that person. What step can you now take to give more of that to yourself?

_____

The next step is to think back to the time when you also showed kindness to someone else. Write now the steps you can take, at least four or five steps that you can take right now to show more kindness to yourself.

_____

Let's think back to the last time when you showed love to someone else. How can you show more of this towards yourself right now? Or what actions can you take you commit to, to give more of this to you right now?

_____

When was the last time you made someone happy or laughed or just cheered them up, and what can you do now? What steps can you take today to make yourself happier?

_____

Now that you've done that, write how you are feeling now out of ten, ten being thrilled and content and then, of course, zero is being really unhappy.

Do you feel or see a shift? If you perhaps don't take a deep breath, because if you commit to what you wrote just now, you will see a shift. That is a promise.

The journey of self-love is not an easy one. It takes a lot of effort, motivation, hard work, and determination. You are basically changing the way your brain was rewired from an early age. It is not a simple task, but you have already come a long way if you have worked on yourself and developed self-love. The moment you decided you needed to explore the topic of self-love was an essential moment in your journey toward self-love.

You paid yourself back for all the effort that you put into the world. Realizing that you needed to develop self-love was one of the most important steps of the many steps that you have to take. But if you have come this far in your journey, then there is no need to hesitate because it is possible for you to achieve self-love.

Do not think of this journey as a one-day task, as it is something that you will develop day by day. Developing self-love is something that you will have to work on every day. But this will be one of the most important journeys of your life.

The more you know yourself, the more you will notice a lot of positive changes in your life. When you develop self-love, you will also feel a lot of positive changes in your relationships with other people. You realize that many negative things in your life were because of your lack of self-love.

On this beautiful journey, you will love yourself slowly and gradually. But with every step you take, you will feel a shift in your life. Self-love will make you flourish in your relationship with your own self, your relationship with other people, your progress in life, and your mental health.

You will learn to appreciate yourself for the efforts you make. You will depend less on other people to meet your emotional needs. It might be difficult to rewire the neural pathways of your brain, but it is not impossible. If you have come this far, do not stop now. Some days might be difficult, but it does not stop them from being beautiful too.

Achieving self-love will help you see the beauty in life. It will make not only your life more positive and happier but also the live of people surrounding you. As you will love yourself, you will find it easier to love other people too. You will be more compassionate towards yourself and other people. The journey of self-love is a beautiful one, and you should be proud of yourself for starting this journey. You are lovable, you matter, and you are enough. Do not let anyone or anything make you believe otherwise.

About the author

Evette Rose is an Author, Life Coach, Metaphysical Anatomy Technique (M.A.T) development company and founder of several books. Evette was born in South Africa and grew up in Namibia, West Africa. She then moved to Australia, lived in Vanuatu and Bali. She is best known for her work in helping people to resolve trauma from their past and freeing them to live successful and fulfilling lives. Evette's work is drawn from her own personal experience of moving from a difficult past into a well-

balanced life and career. Evette's philosophy is that we, as a human race, are not destined to live our lives in pain because of past trauma or abuse. We often suppress our ability to complete or heal trauma naturally. In today's society, we often suppress our pain in order to keep up with life and avoid being left behind. Fortunately, through gentle therapy, this natural internal healing instinct can be restored. Writing her books has helped Evette reach out to other people who need love, support, and someone to relate to. She shares her experiences with the world, hoping it will help people heal and provide encouragement and reassurance when they need it most. Evette now travels the world teaching personal development seminars and continues her research journey. She has been to well over 40 countries and worked with thousands of people!

Refences

https://www.nature.com/articles/s41598-018-34793-x

https://neurosciencenews.com/self-esteem-brain-mapping-7799/

https://www.bbrfoundation.org/blog/self-love-and-what-it-means

https://www.littlewindow.com.au/blog/tips-for-selflove

https://www.medicalnewstoday.com/articles/321309#Moving-away-from-perfectionism

https://www.healthline.com/health/happy-hormone

https://www.healthline.com/health/dopamine-effects

https://www.healthline.com/health/emotional-dependency#in-a-partner

https://www.topdoctors.co.uk/medical-dictionary/emotional-dependence#:~:text=Emotionally%20dependent%20people%20have%20a,the%20ties%20that%20bind%20them.

https://www.heysigmund.com/toxic-people-when-someone-you-love-toxic/

https://www.lifehack.org/596475/how-we-are-confusing-self-love-with-narcissism-in-this-generation

https://www.livehealthymag.com/self-love/

https://affirmpress.com.au/publishing/the-neuroscience-of-self-love/

https://earthtoyou.co/blogs/learn/the-science-behind-learning-to-love-yourself

http://ccare.stanford.edu/uncategorized/the-scientific-benefits-of-self-compassion-infographic/

https://nesslabs.com/self-love

https://www.ncbi.nlm.nih.gov/pmc/articles/PMC4221212/

https://neurosciencenews.com/self-esteem-brain-mapping-7799/

Made in the USA
Coppell, TX
10 October 2024

38484899R00066